# The Book of
# LABYRINTHS
## and MAZES

Silke Vry

Illustrated by
**Finn Dean**

**PRESTEL**

Munich · London · New York

# Let's get started...

It's so nice that you have found
your way here!

---

This book is an:
## Invitation to a special journey!

What do you need to bring along on your trip? Well, you'll need
patience, courage and self-confidence for your journey along
twisting paths. You will take detours, you will need time,
and you will have to move forward without exactly knowing
where the path leads. However, the destination of the journey
will be your ultimate reward.

Do you want to learn more about getting lost? About the
millennia-old fascination with wandering around? Do you
fancy a confusing, charming journey through the world of
labyrinths and mazes? Are you curious about places and
puzzles that are complex, but also amazingly insightful?
Or about winding paths on which you can lose
yourself, but also find yourself?

# Contents

## 'I THINK I'M GOING CRAZY!'

Detours and wrong turns

## WINDING PATHS AS FAR AS THE EYE CAN SEE

Famous labyrinths from history

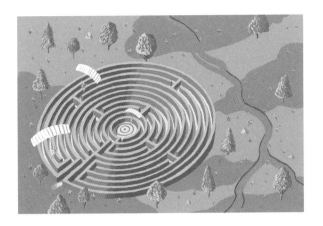

# TO THE CENTER, PLEASE!

But then right back out again!

# STRANGE PATHS!

Mazes all over the world

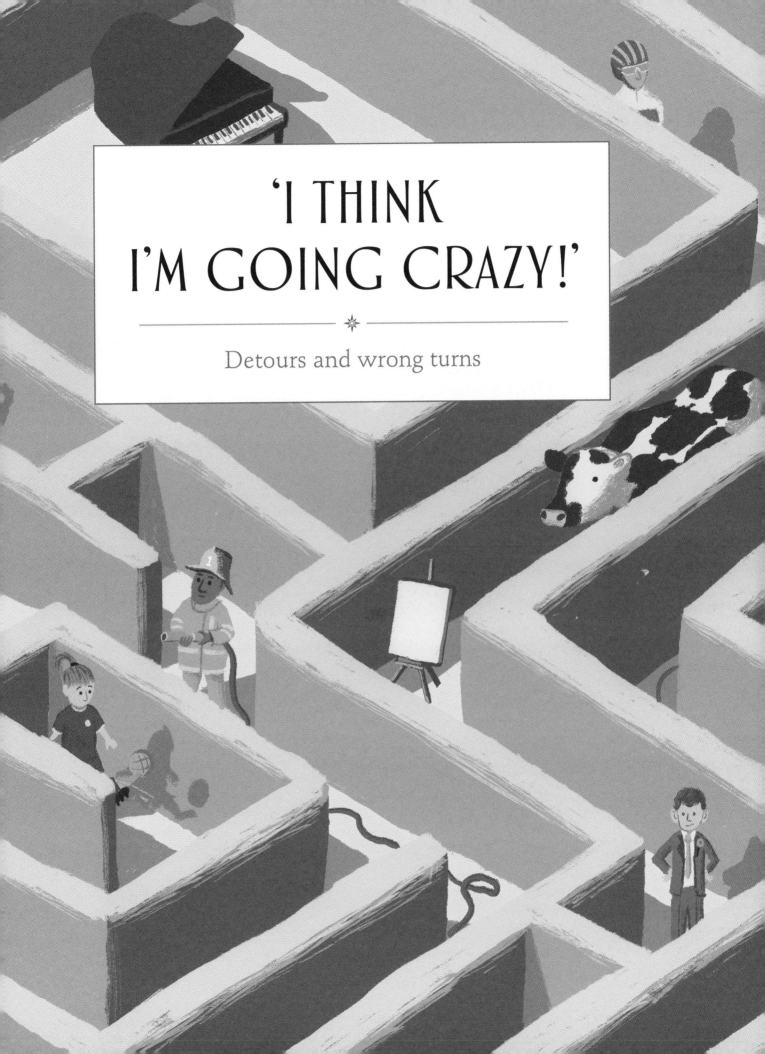

# 'I THINK I'M GOING CRAZY!'

❖

Detours and wrong turns

# A confusing life!

How fast could this happen to someone?
You want to get from one place to another.
That is surely not so difficult, you think, and you
set off through the tangle of streets and alleys.

After a while, you begin to ask yourself:
'Am I going the right way?' It's a hard
question to answer if you do not know
the neighborhood.
You continue to get lost, gear yourself up
and try to be patient in the hope finding
the right path. After a while, at some
time or other, you're forced to admit
that you've 'lost your way'. You must
bravely face the facts: 'I have gotten lost
and I don't know whether I will ever
find myself back on the right track!'
Your forehead may even begin to sweat!

## At such times, you can plainly see:

- ☀ How easy it is to lose your way!

- ☀ How nice and comforting a 'guide' to show you the way would be.

- ☀ How confused you may feel when your destination is no longer in sight.

- ☀ How fantastic inventions such as signposts and satellite navigation systems really are!

### MIND TRIP

When reading this book, try exchanging the word 'way' with 'way of life'. You'll begin to see everything through different eyes, hear the words with different ears and get a completely different understanding of what it means to get lost and to be lost.

# Maze
# or labyrinth?

At the start of our journey through bending paths
and baffling courses, there is one thing you need to know.

### 1.

A labyrinth is not a maze.

### 2.

A maze is therefore not a labyrinth.

### 3.

And – most importantly – you can actually get lost
in a maze (which is not the case in a labyrinth!)

Maze

Labyrinths and mazes have as much in common as astronauts and math teachers, as mustard and mayonnaise, or as 'losing' and 'finding'. They may have similar qualities, but they are quite different!

Compare this labyrinth with this maze. You can see the difference for yourself with a 'finger expedition'. Apart from your finger, all you need is a little bit of creativity and some calm and patience. Just imagine your finger is not a finger... but you, yourself! You will notice many other exciting things as you do this.

One thing is for sure: Labyrinths would not have spread across the whole world and been passed on from person to person unless there was something special about their strangely puzzling routes.

**And that's what this book is also about!**

Labyrinth

# It's crazy! False pathways are everywhere.

Once you've become more acquainted with labyrinths and mazes, you will realize something truly remarkable: **There are false pathways everywhere!** The danger of getting lost and losing your way exists everywhere. And it's often in places we would least expect. These false paths are oftentimes barely visible and even hard to dream up.

Each and every one of us, and mostly of our own free and without losing sleep about it, gets involved in a bit of hustle and bustle. We do not recognize every false trail as a phony detour. Everyday mazes and labyrinths are solely identifiable because they have a beginning and an end. Between the two there is a path we have to tread and endless routes that lead us away from it.

Complex paths exist underground as well. They include the **sewers** that are connected to every house and lie below every street, as well as the jumble of power and telephone cables...

Even 'invisible' things such as **viruses** spread from mouth to mouth and person to person in strange ways. Thankfully, these things can also get stuck at dead-ends – whether it's due to careful hygiene practices or a vaccination.

## Everyday mazes

**When in a city for the first time,** it's easy to get lost within the hubbub of an unfamiliar street and be at constant risk of making a wrong turn.

Objects can also take a wrong turn! Just imagine the **journey a one dollar bill** makes that you yourself have handed out. Where might it be in the evening after you've used it to buy groceries in the morning?

**When surfing the internet,** you very often 'make the wrong turn,' forget why you went online and then fail to find your way back to what you wanted in the first place.

### MIND TRIP

✧

Just imagine if every message sent by our phones left a trail of light behind it. Earth would be covered by an endless, maze-like network!

# Humans – a labyrinth

Were you to take a very close look at a person and peek inside their body, you would discover many surprising things in there. Who would have thought that we ourselves are teeming with labyrinths and false trails?

The labyrinth–like **fingerprint** of one human being is different from all other human beings in the world. At least, that is what we presume until two identical ones are discovered at some point.

The **brain** is a labyrinth with billions of nerve cells. Electric signals race around in this tangled network, which is so complicated that researchers are still discovering things about it today.

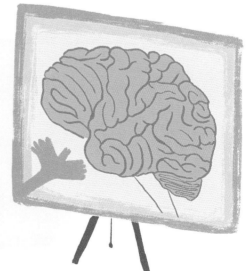

A dense **labyrinth of entrails and intestines** loops about in our stomach. Everyone's looks different. In the past, people regarded this as a 'divine signature' in the bowels. It was even thought that the sacrifice of animal entrails could predict the future.

## MIND TRIP

Anyone who has had their appendix removed might describe their intestine as a 'labyrinth'. Those who still have an appendix might say they possess a 'maze' in their stomach.

The 'labyrinth' in our **ear** consists of a host of twisting passages, ducts and chambers. This inner ear helps us keep our balance and avoid stumbling over our own two feet.

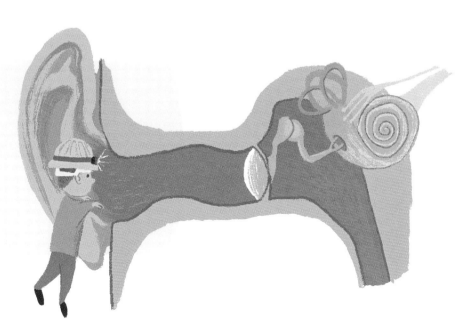

# Making detours, wasting time

Labyrinthine routes are generally not so scary to most people. And detours are usually taken by the ones in a hurry to reach their target in the most direct way possible. People say they never want to 'lose' precious time or be late to an appointment.

## But can you really 'lose' time?

You may be in a hurry, but if you discover something beautiful before you reach your destination, you surely **haven't lost that time**. And you only arrive **'too late'** if you absolutely want to be in a certain place at a certain time (or have to be, – and, admittedly, sometimes you actually have to be).

## Detours, though, are a really great thing.

We far too rarely hear things like:

* Feel free to come to school later today!
* Please go more slowly and dally about!
* Take a detour on your way home.

## MIND TRIP

When we have to take a detour, we often get angry. But instead of getting mad over what seems to be a waste of time, we would be better off concentrating on what we see, get to know, come across and learn on our detours. We might even discover a new goal for our lives – one we'd never have seen when taking a direct course.

'What is the direct course?
The detour.'

**C.G. Jung**

# Moving to the future?

If someone is talking about something that lies in the future or, in other words, about something that is yet to happen, they say: 'That is in front of me!' Yet, if they speak about something that has already happened, something in the past, they say: 'That's behind me.'

This all sounds very normal to us. But if you give it a second thought, you might think: 'Isn't that rather strange?' Does time actually move like someone walking past us on the street?

By the way, people all over the globe do not see the past or the future like this. It's mostly the Western world that believes we move through time – and our own lives – in a straight line.

## MIND TRIP

✦

Try to switch these thoughts around! Imagine that the past is ahead of us and the future behind us. Is it possible to contemplate a future that lies right next to you?

1.

2.

## Your life

In the course of everyone's life, there are two clearly defined points: The moment of birth (A) and the moment of death (B).

1. Will you reach your goal in life quickly and without taking detours, looking over your shoulder or losing time? Will your journey be one without fear, unrest and waywardness?

2. Or does your life send you on a detour? Will you sometimes turn back and start off again toward something new? Will you shun previously trodden pathways and venture along new trails, letting restlessness keep you awake at night and experiencing the unexpected again and again?

# A detour to your goal!

Wandering about can often be an incredible experience – just as long as you don't forget the goal in life that you're actually seeking.

## MIND TRIP

◈

If you were to ask a nomad to talk about his life, he might describe it as a journey of roaming about in curving pathways.

Drifting about can even be helpful and change people's thinking. You may get to know yourself better and get a clearer view of lots of things. You may ask yourself many questions. Did I take a wrong turn sometime in my life? What is the true objective of my journey? Some of these questions may be uncomfortable. Is this the right place for me at all? Will I ever reach my goal?

After such a journey, you will not be the same person at the end as you were in the beginning. That's why there are so many famous stories about wandering about.

# Nature shows us...

Who would have believed this? What many people take for granted in their own lives, namely the straight line connecting one point directly to another without taking a detour, was never nature's intention!

## Straight lines are not natural!

You can look for it as long as you like, but you'll not find a straight line in the natural world. It can't be found in plants or rivers, in animals or clouds, under a microscope or in the orbits of planets in our solar system. We don't even have a single straight line in our own bodies. And there is a simple reason for that. It doesn't make sense in nature!

MARINE FOSSIL

'Beware of the straight line'
is what the Austrian artist
**Friedensreich Hundertwasser.**
once said.

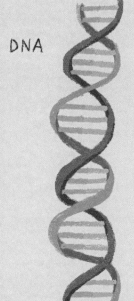

DNA

Things that use 'straight' lines have been invented by humans – from high-rise buildings and modern furniture to subway diagrams and square crispbreads. Nature, on the other hand, is teeming with circles, arcs, waves, twists and curved lines. Nature knows no bounds. And the most common natural form is... well, what do you think?

SNAIL

TORNADO

PINECONE

UNDERSIDE

## MIND TRIP

A puzzling spiral: Giant currents of water and clouds in the Northern Hemisphere twist in a different direction from the ones found in the Southern Hemisphere. The reason for this phenomenon has to do with the way the Earth turns and what is known as the Coriolis force. As the Earth turns eastward, it pushes water and air in a clockwise direction in the north of the planet and the opposite direction in the south.

## It's the spiral!

Spirals seem to rule the natural world. In fact, they have existed everywhere for millions of years. Marine fossils, snail shells, shell trumpets, pine cones, sunflowers, bones, ferns, spider's webs, hair, birds in flight, tornadoes, whirlpools, broccoli… you can find spirals in all of these and in many other plants, animals and natural phenomena. There are spirals in mathematics and, last but not least, in our genetic make-up: our DNA.

Spirals are an ingenious invention of nature. When you hold one in your hand, such as a fresh, young, unfurling leaf, you will be amazed at how flexible and incredibly strong it is!

SPIDER'S WEB

# Magical spirals

Spirals are old, really old! When the first humans appeared on Earth, spirals had already been around for millions of years.

Anyone who has ever found an ammonite or a snail shell will have admired its perfect spiral shape. Some people used to wear them around their necks as a good luck charm. Others saw them as a divine symbol and drew them in sand, painted them on stone or scratched them into hard surfaces.

Around 20,000 years ago, the sign of a spiral had a very special meaning for prehistoric people. It was not just a decoration to make an object look prettier. It was a magical image that possessed the power of prayer or the force of an incantation. The deceased, for example, were buried together with an object with an engraved spiral. It was meant to accompany them on their journey. Just as the spiral had a predetermined path, so too should the dead find their predetermined journey.

## MIND TRIP

Psychology has recognized that spirals can reveal something about people's souls, about their inner being. But the key question is: How do you draw a spiral?

* Anyone who takes a pencil and scribbles inwardly, where things become smaller and smaller until they reach the center, are the ones who look back at their life and focus on what has passed.

* Anyone who starts from the very center and then powerfully draws a circle to the outside are the ones who may look more to the future and see what is to come.

# Spirals and labyrinths

**Spirals** and **labyrinths**
have a lot in common:

- ✸    They both go in one direction.
- ✸    They both have a goal, which lies deep within them.
- ✸    And for both of them, this goal can only be reached in a twisted and roundabout way.

The two are so similar, you would think that if spirals did not exist, then labyrinths would never have been invented.

## MIND TRIP

———— ✦ ————

Like the spiral, the labyrinth is also a
symbol. Its winding paths, with their
constant toing and froing and coming
and going, represent life and the path in
life we have to take, as well as the tasks
and challenges we have to face.

## And yet, there are very interesting differences between them:

✦ A **spiral** always heads in the same direction as you are circling your goal. When you get to the center, you may start to feel dizzy because you have been moving non-stop, round-and-round in the same direction. The path towards the center, in fact, becomes more and more narrow. There is no space for you to easily turn around and find a way back.

✦ There's a big difference when it comes to a **labyrinth**! You'll never get dizzy here because the route in a labyrinth constantly changes its direction. At first, it leads directly to the center. You may think you're arriving at your goal, when the path suddenly takes a big turn. Things then continue that way – sometimes you are very close, sometimes far off the mark. After this emotional roller coaster, you're finally rewarded when you reach the goal. Here you can take a breather, look about, turn around and comfortably make your way out.

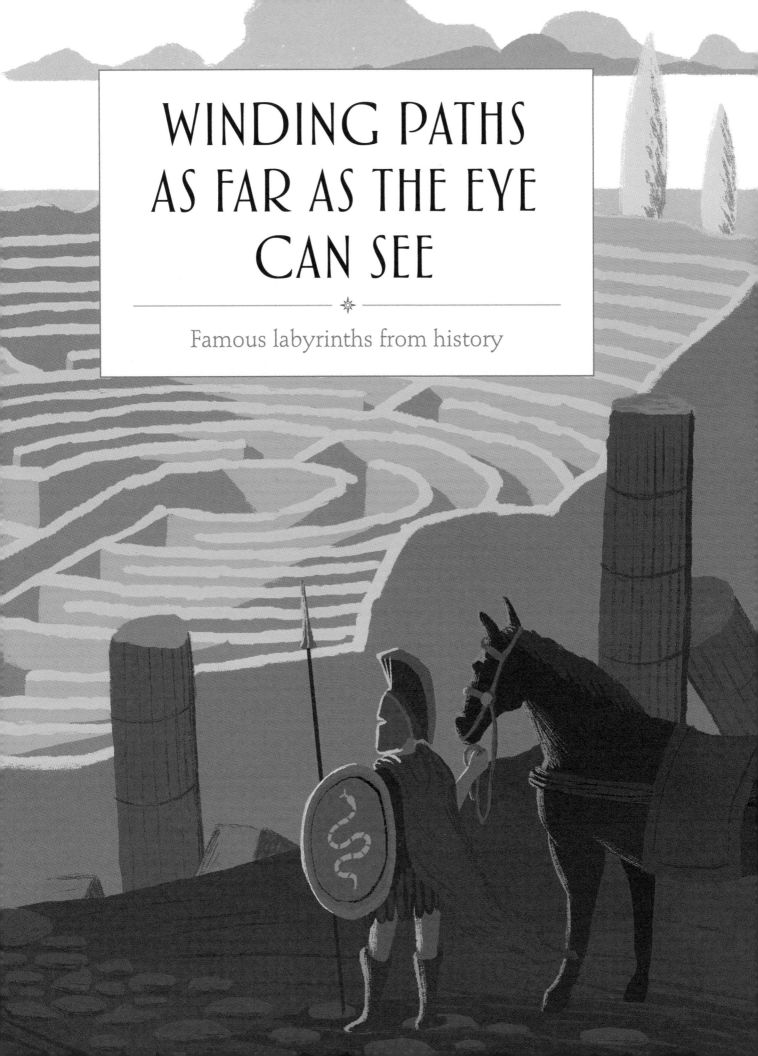

# WINDING PATHS AS FAR AS THE EYE CAN SEE

Famous labyrinths from history

# Theseus and the labyrinth of the Minotaur

A very long time ago, there was a king called Minos, who lived on the island of Crete. King Minos was a wise man and his subjects enjoyed a good and peaceful life during his reign. One day, however, something incredible happened that meant this way of life would never be the same. It all began when the queen gave birth to a terrible monster that was half-bull and half-human. When Minos saw the creature, he wanted to kill it straightaway. His daughter, Princess Ariadne, however, took pity on this unusual being. She asked her father not to kill the Minotaur, the name it had been given by then, but to lock it up instead. The king requested his architect, Daedalus, renowned for his brilliant ideas, to build a prison where the Minotaur would be put away for all time and where it would never be able to find a way out. And that's exactly what happened – Daedalus built a labyrinth!

When the prison was created and the Minotaur caged in it, the people of Crete could live in peace again. The monster, however, needed to be fed, and it preferred to eat humans above all! King Minos had a solution for this dilemma … Every year, seven young men and seven young women had to be brought from

Athens to Crete and sacrificed to the Minotaur! When the Cretans arrived in Athens to collect the 14 young people for a third time, Theseus, the king's son, stood in their way. He wanted to fight the Minotaur, and why not? For it was he who had already defeated giants, monsters, wild animals and an evil sorceress.

When Theseus came to Crete, Princess Ariadne fell madly in love with him. She gave him a gift and explained to him how this gift could save his life. Theseus did as he was told, stormed into the labyrinth, killed the Minotaur and found his way back out with the help of the gift. He then left Crete with Ariadne and the 14 young people and returned to Athens.

✳ You can read more about Ariadne and her enigmatic gift, which showed Theseus the way out of the labyrinth, on page 58.

# A superhero in the labyrinth

What a fabulous story! And it's not over by a long shot. In fact, the story goes on and on and is, in itself, winding and twisted like a never-ending labyrinth – like the path in the life of our hero.

There is hardly anyone other than a hero* who has to endure so many detours and wander throughout the world. For to become a true hero, people like Theseus have to complete all the difficult tasks put in front of them and overcome all dangers and round-about paths.

**A hero's life is anything but swift, straight-forward or even predictable. It is similar to walking through a labyrinth.**

The story of Theseus and the Minotaur did not happen that way in real life... it's a mixture of truth and fantasy, of fears and hopes. But perhaps Theseus' heroic behavior can give us guidance for times when our own path seems confused and aimless.

Like Theseus, we can say to ourselves: ...

* ❋  Be brave!
* ❋  Come on. You can do it!!
* ❋  Go your own way!
* ❋  Know who you are!!

# MIND TRIP

To this day, the mystery of King Minos' labyrinth has never been solved. Archeologists have spent years digging for it, but we still do not know if there really was such a labyrinth on Crete. Were the island's old quarries and ruins in fact the labyrinth? Or was it the confusing and chaotic rooms within the king's palace? How did this strange story of the Minotaur come about? And why?

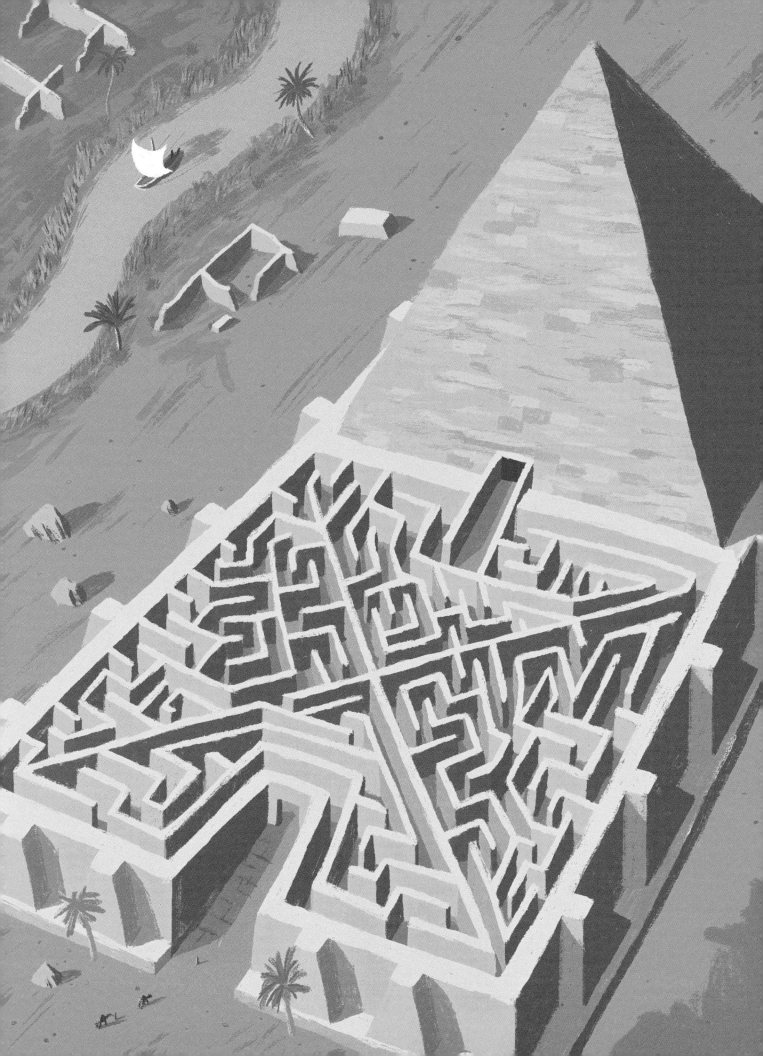

# The labyrinth of the pharaoh

Can you picture a detour so long and confusing that you lose your direction just by looking at it? Does it even make you go insane? Such a labyrinth is said to have existed in ancient Egypt: the mortuary temple of Pharaoh Amenemhet III.

The ancient Greeks acknowledged this labyrinth as a wonder of the world. There was nothing quite like it anywhere else!

The building consisted of 12 palaces with a total of 3,000 rooms and halls, countless columns, interwoven corridors, courtyards and even more pillared hallways. Gods were worshiped in the rooms above ground and in the rooms below ground were crocodiles! Anyone who managed to walk through all of that would arrive at the Amenemhet's great pyramid.

But why was this masterpiece of madness built? Well, the reason is clear. It was to protect the dead pharaoh and his pyramid. Anyone, who entered the building and did not know the labyrinth's plan would go astray and get hopelessly lost. It was a clever way to fend off tomb raiders!

## MIND TRIP

The very idea of getting lost in Amenemhet's dark corridors put off most looters. However, this elaborate security plan didn't work out forever. Archaeologists discovered that the pharaoh's burial chamber had indeed been plundered at some point.

# Labyrinths around the world

**People have been fascinated by labyrinths throughout generations, centuries and millennia. Where, however, was the first labyrinth built and who invented it?**

Labyrinth researchers have been unable to find clear answers to these questions. Only one thing seems certain – no 'original' labyrinth was built at a single place and then copied elsewhere around the world. Labyrinths were developed at different locations by different cultures. It seems that people all over the world had a need to walk, dance and stroll along tangled paths thousands of years ago.

Coins showing labyrinths first appear in **Greece**, where the saga of the Minotaur was born. The oldest known drawing of a labyrinth also comes from Greece. It appears on a clay tablet and is about 3,200 years old.

The ancient **Romans** loved angular labyrinths, which they used as beautiful decoration in villas and spas

In **Asia**, labyrinths appeared in such places as Persia, Afghanistan and India. In India, a labyrinth mirrored the seven twisting paths an unborn baby needed to take in its mother's womb during childbirth. In order for the baby to find its way to the outside, a labyrinth was sketched in a bowl using spices. The bowl was then filled with water, which was drunk by the pregnant mother. In some parts of India, this practice continues today.

Ancient images of labyrinths etched in stone were found in **North America**. The Hopi peoples told a story about the creation of humans and how a legendary hero led them to the Earth's surface from an underground labyrinth. In this culture, labyrinths are still used as symbols on grass baskets and jewelry.

During the European **Middle Ages**, after the fall of the Roman Empire, countless labyrinths were made to decorate the floors of newly erected churches. Medieval Christians said that Jesus was the 'new Theseus' and that he too had saved people from evil (see page 49). Only a few of these labyrinths have survived. The best known example is the one in the Cathedral of Chartres in France. Pilgrims still cross through such labyrinths on their knees during short religious visits. The labyrinth on pages 50/51 has the same shape as the Chartres labyrinth.

In **England** and other European countries, churches were often quite small, so labyrinths would be made in the lawns next to them. Remarkably, some of these 'garden' labyrinths have survived the centuries almost unharmed. Seven of them remain in England and three in Germany, one of which can be found in Hanover.

Almost every King of **France** was crowned at Reims Cathedral, where they would cross over the great labyrinth on their way to the throne on coronation day.

In 1815, German settlers planted a labyrinth in their new American homeland, a small town called New Harmony in Indiana, USA. These people had left a difficult life path behind them in Germany, and now they faced just as difficult a journey in their adopted country. Their labyrinth was meant to show them the twisting path of life and give them hope.

## And today?

Our world is full of crazy paths and intersections, where we have to choose which particular trail we need to follow. How often would you wish for a signpost to help direct you towards your goal?

Nowadays, people stressed by everyday life seek distraction and relaxation in modern labyrinths and mazes, which are enjoying great popularity. Maybe you've been to a labyrinth yourself? Or to an escape room, which is a very special kind of maze?

# Magical labyrinths

## People have always believed in the magical and health-giving powers of labyrinths.

In 1924, people aboard the first scheduled flight to go over the Nazca desert in Peru witnessed an amazing sight. As they looked out their windows, they saw down below labyrinthine lines, mysterious signs, miles-long layers of stone, crazy pathways and huge pictures in the sand. These vast and confusing man-made creations have preoccupied scientists ever since. The lines in the earth probably originated more than 2,000 years ago, when there was a major drought in the area. Perhaps the people living there had walked the winding paths between the stone layers to ask the gods for rain?

In Ancient Greece, sick people often came to one of the largest and most advanced 'hospitals' of the time. It was the Asclepius Sanctuary in Epidaurus. Archeologists discovered an underground labyrinth while excavating the grounds of the site. What was it used for? Scientists believe that Asclepius priests descended into the 'underworld' with the ill people so they could make their way across the paths of the labyrinth – something that was considered a form of healing in those days!

## MIND TRIP

Healers already knew thousands of years ago that walking in labyrinths can make you healthy. It can't cure the worst illnesses, of course, but it can help people feel more relaxed and soothe their souls.

# The 'new Theseus'

**Walking through a labyrinth is a special experience that can inspire people to think more deeply about their own life, about God and about the world.**

The story of Theseus and Ariadne was known far and wide over 2,000 years ago – how Theseus defeated wickedness inside the labyrinth, how Ariadne helped him get out and how the two of them made the world a better place.

When Christianity emerged, Jesus was called the 'New Theseus' because he was actually a hero, too. Like Theseus, Christ also put his life on the line, died, was resurrected and made a gift to humankind of 'eternal life' after death.

And that is how the labyrinth became a Christian symbol. The winding paths were an image of a confusing, evil world. The labyrinth fitted in well with all the healing stories the Christian church had to tell, and its churches were suddenly teeming with twisting routes and trails! Medieval people, in fact, were supposed to pass through them when they visited church.

## MIND TRIP
✦

'Finger labyrinths' have been preserved within the entrances to some medieval churches even to this day. Barely larger than a family pizza and positioned at eye-level, they helped you get into the right mood for the church service.

# Secret symbols and magical numbers

The Christian world of the Middle Ages
(from about 500 – 1,500 AD) was full
of symbols and religious images.
And there was a practical reason for
this. Most people could not read,
but they could learn from pictures,
shapes and numeric signs –
including those found in
labyrinths.

**Circle:** The circle has always
stood for perfection. Many
churches favored circular
labyrinths.

**Cross:** Jesus died on a cross,
but the cross is also a symbol
for Christ's resurrection. Every
church maze, whether eight-
sided or circular, contains the
shape of a cross.

**Octagon:** Eight is thought to be a special number. The geometrical shape of the octagon, for example, is seen as perfect and can be found in baptismal fonts. Many Christian labyrinths are shaped as a figure eight.

**Eleven bends:** Nearly all labyrinths of this time have eleven circular curves. The number eleven stands for both 'excess' and 'imperfection'. Eleven is more than the perfect ten (with its 'ten commandments'), but cannot match up to the wonderful twelve (with its 'twelve disciples'). The eleven courses of the labyrinth, as well as the labyrinth itself, symbolize the earthly world with all its imperfections.

**Twenty-eight intersections:** The earthly number four (think of the four seasons or the four cardinal points on a compass) multiplied by seven, the perfect number (not only in Christianity, but also in other religions), equals 28. Twenty eight is also the number of turning points that exist in medieval labyrinths. At these points it is made clear: 'Turn back! Change the direction of your life path! Only when you turn around will you begin to reach your goal!'

Which symbols can you spot in this labyrinth?

# In the labyrinth of words

## Who would have thought that words, letters and whole sentences could go on detours?

You read with your eyes working left to right, which can be something of a strain. You have to recognize all the letters, interpret them, put them into a sensible word, string them all together as a sentence and then compile the sentences into a meaningful chapter.

Is that not enough? Could reading be even more complicated? Well, yes it can, and the idea is very, very old indeed.

At some point or other in the past, someone came up with the idea of having written words run as a spiral or even as labyrinths. What was the reason for that? Well, it's very simple. People, who used to read serious, educational or sad texts, as well as prayers or extracts from the bible, were meant to work hard and make an effort when they read. After all, reading this type of text was not for entertainment. How things have changed nowadays!

WATCH YOUR CHARACTER. WATCH YOUR CHARACTER, FOR IT BECOMES YOUR DESTINY

WATCH YOUR WORDS, THEY BECOME ACTIONS.

WATCH YOUR ACTIONS, THEY BECOME HABITS,

WATCH YOUR HABITS, THEY BECOME CHARACTER.

## MIND TRIPS

✦

Just imagine there is a maze of letters, where individual words are an intersection amid other labyrinth letters. Does that sound complicated? It is, and it has been around for a long time. We even have our own word mazes today. Think about hyperlinks on the internet – the short cuts, cross-references and intersections that tie every imaginable word to another.

Particularly exciting stories can sometimes be structured like a maze. The main character makes a decision that sets many different aspects of the story in motion. Should another decision have been made, the tale could have gone off in a completely opposite direction.

# TO THE CENTER, PLEASE!

But then right back out again!

# The path is the target

Anyone entering a labyrinth is looking for something.
You are looking for a goal. You are looking for the center.

At first glance, this task doesn't seem too difficult.
You cannot possibly get lost because there is only one
path. No matter whether you walk quickly, calmly,
with focus or with a bounce, you will reach your goal
at some point. However, you can discover much more
than just the center in a labyrinth…

**Right then! What else?**

MIND TRIP

✦

The imaginary trips people make when passing through a labyrinth are as varied as the labyrinths themselves.

The path through a labyrinth can be long and arduous. You may suffer disappointments, get impatient, sense hope and believe you are nearly at the target, only to have to turn around again. You begin to understand everything from a different standpoint. Hopefully, you'll soon manage to loosen up and calm down. On this journey, you are suddenly aware of not only the labyrinth itself, but also of your thoughts, feelings and life. You discover yourself!

People experience and learn something very special when they enter a labyrinth and travel through it. Labyrinths are more than just a pastime:

**A labyrinth helps inspire thoughts and ideas, and you can learn a lot from the experience.**

* 'Never stop, even if it seems there is no way to carry on!'
* 'The path leads to the goal!'
* 'Don't worry. You can hardly make any mistakes.'
* 'Don't be afraid, even if something changes!'

# Ariadne! Help!

If you think back to the puzzling story of Theseus, the Minotaur and Ariadne on pages 34/35, you may remember that it did not mention what kind of gift Ariadne gave to her beloved Theseus so he could leave the labyrinth unharmed.

This gift was nothing more than a: **ball of thread!** Theseus unraveled the thread as he stormed his way into the labyrinth so that he could find his way back to the exit.

But isn't that rather odd? If there is only one way to the center of the labyrinth, there can only be one way back out. Why would Theseus need the thread to find his way back?

## MIND TRIP

It's hard to say why Ariadne gave the thread as a gift. It's just as difficult to explain why Theseus did not refuse it. What kind of hero needs thread to find his way out of a labyrinth? The answer could be that the labyrinth looked much different from the way we think it did. Maybe it was much more complicated? Or maybe the thread – like so many things in labyrinths – was a symbol for something totally different? Who knows?

It's not by chance, of course, that thread has always had
a special meaning in many cultures.

**Do you know these expressions?**

* 'I lost my thread …'
* 'Your essay has no common thread!'
* 'His thread of life was cut short.'
* 'His life is hanging by a thread.'

With the ancient Greeks, 'thread' always meant fate. When a person
was born, the goddesses of fate spun a thread that contained everything
a person was to expect during his journey in life – it was his fate.
Once the thread was ready, it was cut off at a specific point.
According to this idea, a person's lifetime was already mapped out
from their day of birth.

There is a belief in China that men and women destined to be married
to each other are connected by a red thread at their ankles.

# Tangled paths

Whether drawn on paper, pressed into the sand or stamped out in the snow, labyrinths serve their purpose. You will find your way to the center no matter what!

Try making your own labyrinths:

Even a wild scribble can produce the most beautiful labyrinth. Don't forget to mark the beginning with 'Start' and the end with 'Finish'.

START

FINISH

For a simple round labyrinth, you will need six circles. Begin with the smallest one and then draw the next, larger-sized circles around each other. Mark an entrance as a starting point and the center as the target. Now, erase a space to create a passage from each of the circles, and in such a way that makes the labyrinth rich in detours...

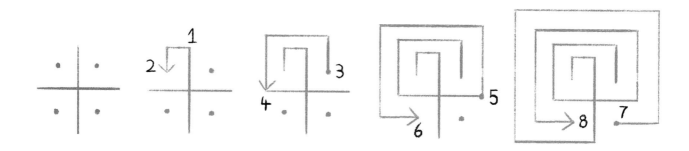

This is how you draw a simple, three-way labyrinth.
Begin with a cross and add a dot at each intersection.
Then join up the points as illustrated here.

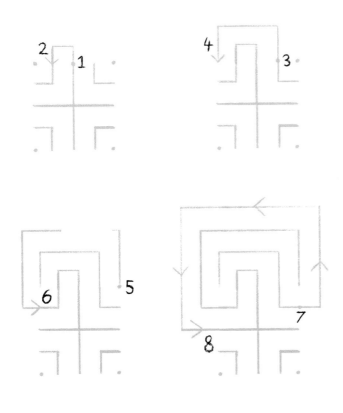

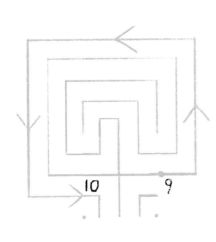

The next labyrinth can be created in a similar way, but with a small change. After drawing the cross, add right-angle corners to each intersection and only then add a dot. Continue as shown.

Try to add more right angles to get more detours.

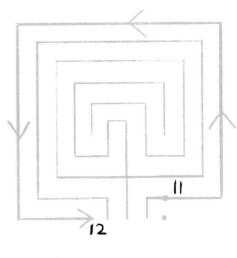

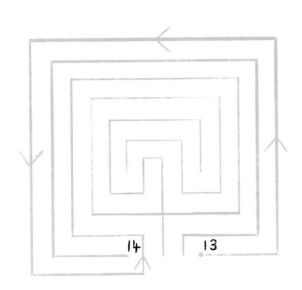

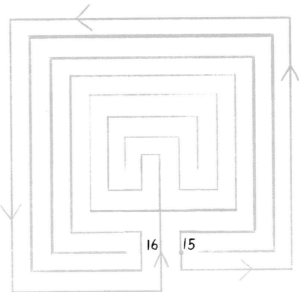

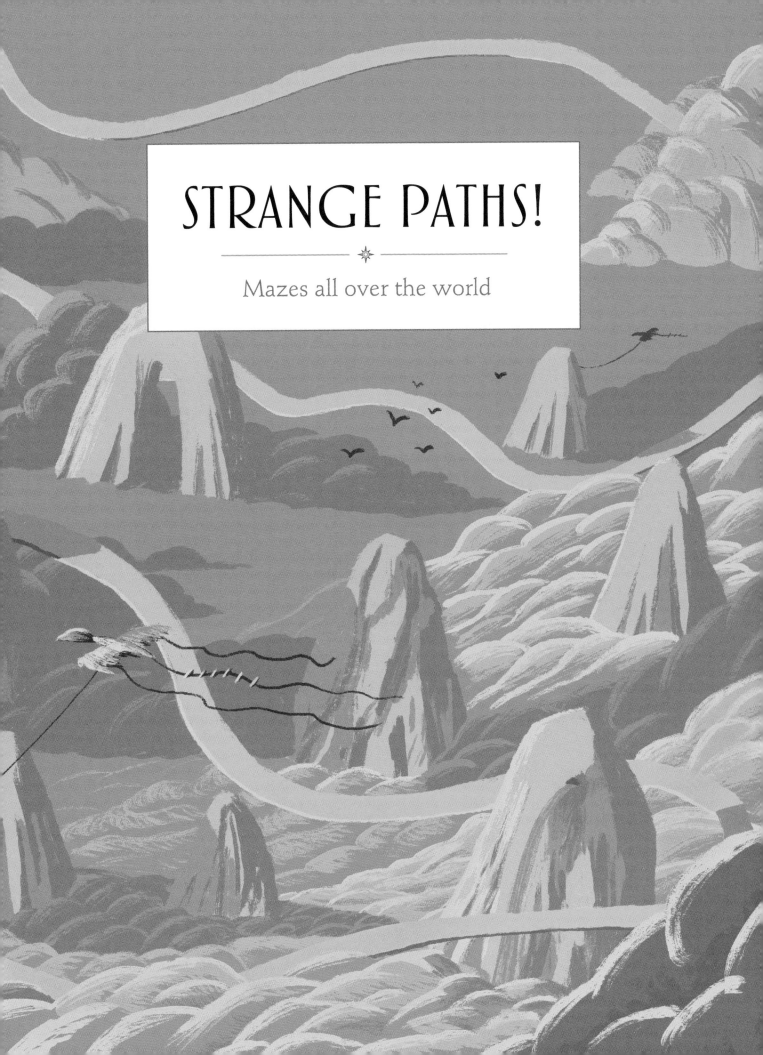

# STRANGE PATHS!

Mazes all over the world

# From a labyrinth to a maze

About 500 years ago, European rulers (kings, counts and dukes) began to make their gardens more decorative by building labyrinths in their palaces and castles. And what a clever idea it was! They built them out of hedgerows!

Enthusiastic court guests strolled through these gardens under sunny skies, on soft soil and amidst fragrant greenery. What fun! Nobody would have had any concern other than pastime and pleasure. They certainly wouldn't have been inspired to contemplate their own emotional or spiritual 'center'.

Over time, court gardeners began altering the labyrinths to make them more amusing. They removed a little tree here, blocked off a path there and created dead-ends. By doing these things, they transformed the labyrinths into something new: the first mazes.

## MIND TRIP

———— ✦ ————

It doesn't take all that much to change a labyrinth into a maze. Take a quick look at the plain, round labyrinth on page 60. Is this a labyrinth or is it really a maze? What would happen if you added even more passages?

# Landscaped fun and confusion

Some rulers, such as kings and queens, wanted to offer their guests even more fun on their confused stroll through planted hedges and walkways. They decorated their mazes with statues of dwarfs, mythical creatures and monsters.

This meant that walking through a maze was not only entertaining, but also informative: 'Just look at what dangers are lurking about when you end up on the wrong path!' is what these images were meant to illustrate.

Between 1756 and 1759, Emperor Qianlong of China had a maze built in his palace in Peking. He loved to sit on his raised pavilion on warm summer evenings and watch his guests wander about with little lanterns.

# A decision needs to be made!

**About 500 years ago, when mazes became popular, a lot was changing in the world.**

Philosophers, thinkers and scientists began to explore the world and make discoveries. There were new ideas in science, history, philosophy and art. For a long time, strict religious rules had determined people's lives. But now, new ideas were spreading. People not only wanted to focus on the salvation of their souls after death, they also attached meaning to a good life in the here and now. People suddenly felt themselves to be the 'measure of all things', and that was a completely new way of thinking.

For centuries, people had regarded the life path of a person like that of a labyrinth – unavoidably predetermined.

But now the maze helped make a new idea clear to people: one could decide for oneself, in certain situations, what path to take in life. One, in fact, MUST decide for oneself about something new when a fork in the road appears.

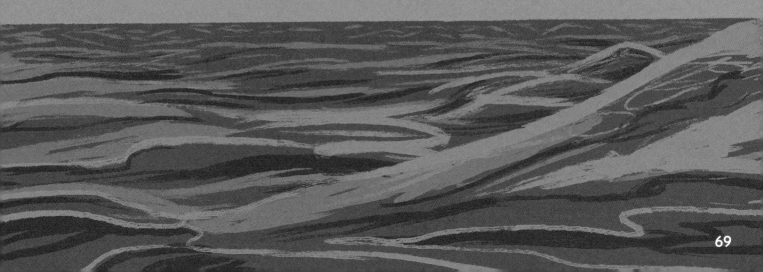

# Going crazy
## on crazy paths...

You need staying power and, above all, patience to get through a labyrinth. You will not miss out on your goal because there is only one way to the center. Going into a maze, however, is a different story entirely.

If you run your finger through this maze, you will rather quickly and easily make your way out of it. Why is that so? Well, it's quite simple: Because you're looking from above at the winding corridors, pathways, and dead-ends, you can easily see everything that matters. You have the overview. You know exactly where you have come from, where you want to go and which turn-offs you should avoid. But if you enter a maze with your whole body and from ground level, you don't have such a perfect overview. Your eye only makes out a part of the path obscured by walls of hedges and leaves.

You can experience this feeling of getting lost in a maze without leaving your house. First, draw a simple maze on a piece of paper. Next, cut a hole in the middle of another piece of paper and place the paper above the maze. You can now 'travel' along the maze while looking through the hole. By doing so, you'll experience the disorienting, limited view that you would have on a real walk through a maze.

**If you compare a maze with a labyrinth, you will notice:**

* A maze forces you to make decisions at intersections.
* In a maze, you have to trust in luck and good fortune to do the right thing.
* If you lose your overview in a maze, you lose sight of your goal.
* You can maintain your hold of the overview using a great sense of direction and your own imagination.
* You are constantly looking for the exit in a maze.
* You don't gain much by going through a maze, but you may lose something – first your calm and later your mind!

One thing is quite possible:
**A maze can make you crazy!**

# Typical maze!

The **entrance** is often the **exit**. This is confusing because the start is also the target. Before you enter the maze, you already have the target before your very eyes. (1)

One **path can fork** and every intersection seems like a new main route. You are the one who has to decide which path to choose. (2)

There is a **central point that** can be designed as an elevated lookout. You can take a breather here and often get an overview. But things may not be so easy as you make your way back and try (sometimes for hours) to find the exit. (3)

There are **changes in direction**. In your confusion, you may not even realize this. Their only purpose in a maze is to create further confusion, not to gain personal knowledge as in a labyrinth. (4)

Sometimes, there are **small statues** at the intersections, which are meant to help you decide where to go. Is it better to head in the direction where the statue of 'wickedness' is located or where the statue of 'virtue' stands? (The answer, of course, is usually the statue of 'virtue'!) (5)

# Losing your way in life

Life itself can be like walking through a maze. All of us are faced with making decisions every now and again. Sometimes, they can be very difficult! It's as if you were standing at an intersection in the road and have to decide which way to go – right or left – without knowing what to expect.

Maybe you will regret some of your choices and say to yourself: If only I had gone to ballet lessons instead of that stupid soccer club, I might now be the star performer at the national opera!

In your mind, you can always go back to the crossroads where you had to decide: left, ballet; right, soccer. On the way back, however, you would have to give thought to all those things you might have missed had you decided differently – being friends with star players, the fantastic soccer boots and loads of other things.

You may well get annoyed about this missed intersection and believe you chose the wrong path. Even at the next crossroads, you may get doubts because you believe you have always chosen unwisely. Within the maze of life, it's possible to go crazy!

## MIND TRIP

It's interesting to chat with elderly people. What does the maze of a long life look like? Were there forks in the road where they would have preferred to take a different path? Where would their life have led them? Perhaps you may also discover that their choices were exactly right for them. 'At no point,' they might say, 'did I have any difficulty in making a decision. An inner voice was guiding me. I would never have wanted to go any other way.' Their life had given them something different than a maze. It had given them a labyrinth!

'There are no signposts at the crossroads of life'
Charlie Chaplin

# Lost!

"Harris asked me if I'd ever been in the maze at Hampton Court. He said he went in once to show somebody else the way. He had studied it up in a map, and it was so simple that it seemed foolish – hardly worth the twopence charged for admission. Harris said he thought that map must have been got up as a practical joke, because it wasn't a bit like the real thing, and only misleading. It was a country cousin that Harris took in. He said: 'We'll just go in here, so that you can say you've been, but it's very simple. It's absurd to call it a maze. **You keep on taking the first turning to the right.** We'll just walk round for ten minutes, and then go and get some lunch.'

They met some people soon after they had got inside, who said they had been there for three-quarters of an hour, and had had about enough of it. Harris told them they could follow him, if they liked; he was just going in, and then should turn round and come out again. They said it was very kind of him, and fell behind, and followed.

They picked up various other people who wanted to get it over, as they went along, until they had absorbed all the persons in the maze. People who had given up all hopes of ever getting either in or out, or of ever seeing their home and friends again, plucked up courage at the sight of Harris and his party, and joined the procession, blessing him. Harris said he should judge there must have been twenty people following him, in all; and one woman with a baby, who had been there all the morning, insisted on taking his arm, for fear of losing him.

Harris kept on turning to the right, but it seemed a long way, and his cousin said he supposed it was a very big maze.

'Oh, one of the largest in Europe,' said Harris.

'Yes, it must be,' replied the cousin, 'because we've walked a good two miles already.'

Harris began to think it rather strange himself, but he held on until, at last, they passed the half of a penny bun on the ground that Harris's cousin swore he had noticed there seven minutes ago. Harris said: 'Oh, impossible!' But the woman with the baby said, 'Not at all,' as she herself had taken it from the child, and thrown it down there, just before she met Harris. She also added that she wished she never had met Harris, and expressed an opinion that he was an impostor. That made Harris mad, and he produced his map, and explained his theory.

'The map may be all right enough,' said one of the party, 'if you know whereabouts in it we are now.'

Harris didn't know, and suggested that the best thing to do would be to go back to the entrance, and begin again. For the beginning again part of it there was not much enthusiasm; but with regard to the advisability of going back to the entrance there was complete unanimity, and so they turned, and trailed after Harris again, in the opposite direction. About ten minutes more passed, and then they found themselves in the centre.

Harris thought at first of pretending that that was what he had been aiming at; but the crowd looked dangerous, and he decided to treat it as an accident.

Anyhow, they had got something to start from then. They did know where they were, and the map was once more consulted, and the thing seemed simpler than ever, and off they started for the third time.

And three minutes later they were back in the centre again.

After that, they simply couldn't get anywhere else. Whatever way they turned brought them back to the middle. It became so regular at length, that some of the people stopped there, and waited for the others to take a walk round, and come back to them. Harris drew out his map again, after a while, but the sight of it only infuriated the mob, and they told him to go and curl his hair with it. Harris said that he couldn't help feeling that, to a certain extent, he had become unpopular."

(Passage from "Three Men in a Boat", chapter VI, by Jerome K. Jerome. 1889)

# Getting back

This story shows how easy it is to underestimate a maze.
People who are lost and confused often find life difficult.
Being confused means the exact opposite of 'having a clear head'.
Harris' idea about finding his way back to the entrance only
to start everything off afresh shows that he is not just lost
but rather confused.

**Confused:** Is Harris correct in his belief that you should always stick to the right at every turn-off in the maze to be sure to find your way out? He seems very convinced about that.

**Confused:** Why doesn't Harris simply guide his friends out of the labyrinth by using his map? Surely, if you have a map in hand, you should always be able to find your bearings. Or maybe not?

**Unraveled:** Harris is partly correct. However, if you start using this idea after you've already gotten lost, then it's too late! You can try out Harris' method yourself by running your finger around the overview of the maze at Hampton Court (see pages 78/79).

**Unraveled:** No, of course you can't, because you would first need to know exactly where you are located in the maze. And that is exactly what Harris does not know. A map in moments like this is of no use to anybody.

To find out more about this 'hand method', check out pages 82/83.

To be honest, Harris and his new 'friends' in
the story never find their way out of the maze.
Instead, they call the park warden for help, but
even the warden himself is not that smart and also
gets lost in the maze. It's only a second warden
who manages to guide everybody out. The map
did not help them much because they were unable
to get any sense of 'orientation' from it.

# Instruction manual
# for mazes

## Before entering a maze, there are a few things you should know...

* Without a plan (followed from the very beginning), only good luck will get you through. But good luck should not be underestimated!
* A good memory, which you should train before entering the maze, would also be an advantage, but it's by no means a guarantee.
* Try, try and keep on trying! Look to the left, look to the right, hope, go with the flow and rely on good fortune. Anyone able to do all of this will get through the maze without going completely crazy.

# You need to remember one of these escape plans no matter what:

## The hand method:

When you go into a maze, always keep your hand brushed against one of the walls and never, ever let go. (This method almost always works!).

## The Tarry method:

As soon as you enter a passage in a maze, mark it with the sign 'Stop'. You will now never go into a passage a second time if it is marked 'Stop'. If you come to a crossroads that you have never been to before and its passages are not marked, then mark the passage you have just come from with the sign: 'Last'. Next, choose any passage to move forwards. Should you only arrive at marked passages, then go into the one marked 'Last'. This way, you're guaranteed to end up at the exit.

At some stage, of course, you will definitely find your way out of a maze, whether with a map or a method.

But what is it like with the mazes of life? What is the solution? Who is going to give you Ariadne's thread, which you sorely need when your school paper seems to be a labyrinth of single words and when math appears to be one false path taking you to unknown regions?

What then? Maybe you can ask a special person for some advice or just rely on what you feel inside to show you the right path?

Let only those into your labyrinth
who carry hope in their hands
and tenderness in their eyes,
do not measure the day by hours
and open up their hearts to magic
behind the apparitions
and completely forget
to look for the exit.

**Irish Blessing**

# Drawing mazes

For a simple maze, draw a squiggly line
and then another above it.
Then, choose a start and a finish.

START

FINISH

This image shows the very first 'maze' ever
drawn, and it's about 600 years old. It was made
by an Italian doctor, Giovanni Fontana, who had
no intention of pleasing or entertaining anyone
whatsoever. His maze (not made out of hedges
but of walls) was meant to be a jailhouse for
criminals. That's why there is no exit, but only
an entrance and door that could be locked.

# To construct a maze:

FINISH

START

**1.**
Settle on the space that you'll need to create the maze. Mark the start and the finish.

**2.**
Decide on a uniform type of pathway. Should the maze be made up of straight lines or curved ones?

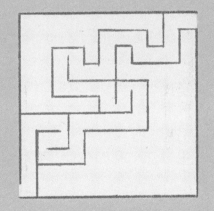

• **3.**
Now, draw from the start the route that will lead to the finish.

**4.**
Only after you've finished these steps can you add in the dead ends.
(Please note: More often than not, maze-goers travel toward the right rather than the left, so there should be fewer dead-ends leading off to the right! Also, try to keep the area between the passage and open spaces the same size.)

# Confusing and strange

Labyrinths have existed around the world for thousands of years, and they all bear a remarkable resemblance to each other.

A knot is like a labyrinth. And even a knot seems to hide a secret. Whenever someone solves a problem, we often say they have 'unraveled the knot'!

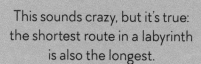

This sounds crazy, but it's true: the shortest route in a labyrinth is also the longest.

It's interesting to note how the word 'maze' is defined differently in other languages. 'Maze' in English originates from the word 'amaze'. However, it is also 'amazing' that many other languages do not make a distinction between mazes and labyrinths, and that some do not even have their own word for maze!

In the first intelligence tests carried out on rats around 1920, the animals were supposed to find their way out of a small maze designed like the one in Hampton Court. The researchers quickly discovered that this maze was too difficult even for intelligent rats! They also found out that the older the rats were, the more difficulties they had trying to make their way out of the maze.

After winning his fight against the Minotaur, Theseus traveled to the island of Delos. Once there, he danced the 'Geranos' with his companions. The 'Geranos' crane dance is performed in a circle and describes in spiral-shaped lines what passing through and coming out of a labyrinth is like. This type of dancing in a circle is still performed all around the Mediterranean to this day, not just in Greece!

It used to be customary for seafarers in Scotland and Sweden to pass through a labyrinth made of stone before boarding their boats. This was meant to drive away the dangers they faced during the trip and return them home with good fortune after their wandering about at sea.

In China and India, labyrinths are painted on the roofs of houses. This is meant to ward off evil spirits. According to legend, spirits are unable to penetrate a labyrinth because they only move in straight lines!

Scientists have discovered that even running your finger through a labyrinth has a strongly calming effect. For example, if you photocopy the labyrinth on the left and then repeatedly run your finger through it when you are feeling restless or 'beside yourself', the labyrinth will work its powers and help you find your center again.

# The labyrinths and mazes in this book

Numbers in bold refer to pages with illustrations

### The labyrinth of the Minotaur

P. 34–**37**, 58

The heroic tale of Theseus features this legendary labyrinth on Crete. However, we do not know what it looked like or if it actually existed. All the 'images' we have of it come from peoples' imagination.

### Labyrinth of pharaoh Amenemhet III

P. **38**/39

This ancient Egyptian king reigned around 1800 BC. He built his burial temple in Hawara, Egypt, with a labyrinth to protect it from grave robbers. In the long run, however, this defense system did not work and the tomb was plundered. No one knows exactly what the labyrinth looked like, so our illustrator created an imaginary picture of it.

### Labyrinth on a Roman floor mosaic

P. **41**

This illustration is inspired by a floor mosaic from a Roman villa found in Cremona, Italy. The mosaic is now displayed in the Cremona Archaeological Museum.

### Labyrinth at Chartres Cathedral

P. 43, **50**/**51**

The labyrinth at the cathedral in Chartres, France, was built at the beginning of the 13th century. It has a diameter of about 42 feet (13 meters), a pathway about 13 inches (34 cm) wide and a total pathway length of about 850 feet (260 meters). The path through this labyrinth turns at six points at a 90-degree angle to the left and to the right. In fact, it even makes a 180-degree turn 28 times and returns in the direction from which it started.

### Labyrinth at Reims Cathedral

P. **43**

Nearly every French king was crowned in this cathedral. The labyrinth here was set down in the church floor in 1286 but then later removed by church officials some 500 years later. The reason is said to have been children who were noisily enjoying the labyrinth and disturbing those praying in the building. Sadly, it was never restored, yet we know what it looked like. An image of the Reims labyrinth now serves as the logo used to mark significant French monuments.

### Labyrinth in New Harmony

P. **44**

This labyrinth was built in a town in the U.S. state of Indiana. The town was founded by German immigrants in the early 1800s.

### Labyrinth in the Nazca desert

P. **46**/47

The Nazca Lines are huge images made of stones that are only recognizable from the sky above. They date from around 500 BC to 500 AD. Numerous archaeologists have studied them. The figures probably had a cultural meaning, and they may have been a place where religious celebration took place. Our picture shows the image of a monkey.

## The Sanctuary of Asclepius in Epidaurus

P. 47

In ancient times, this was one of the most important shrines in Ancient Greece. Asclepius, the Greek god of healing, was worshipped here. The sanctuary also served as a hospital, and its labyrinth was located underneath the beautiful rotunda, or Tholos.

## The labyrinth of Amiens

P. 48

This image shows the labyrinth in the Gothic cathedral of Amiens, France. The octagonal labyrinth was laid down with stones in the floor of the church in 1288. It was rebuilt from 1894 to 1897 using a model of the destroyed original, and it measures 39 by 49 feet (12 by 15 meters).

## The maze in Somerleyton Gardens

P. 64/65

In 1846, a geometric maze was planted in a corner of the Victorian manor house of Somerleyton in the east of England. This maze inspired our illustrator to create the image on pages 64 and 65.

## The labyrinth in the palace of Emperor Qianlong, Beijing

P. 66/67

In 1747, the Chinese emperor had this maze built along the lines of the maze at Versailles Palace in France.

## The maze in Glendurgan Garden

P. 72/73

An example of the many beautiful English hedge mazes is at Glendurgan Garden in England's Cornwall region. It was landscaped in the garden in 1822.

## Hampton Court maze

P. 76–79

This maze is part of the royal palace by the Thames in west London. At 1,650 square yards (1,380 square meters), it is relatively small. In theory, you could reach the center in just a few minutes. Visitors, however, usually spend an average of 90 minutes here. In earlier years, researchers used a floor plan of this maze in experiments with rats.

## Labyrinth of Giovanni Fontana

P. 84

Fontana (1395–1455) was an Italian medical practitioner and author. He resided in Crete for a while, and perhaps that's where he got the idea for a labyrinth where you could really get lost.

# Discovering labyrinths and mazes for yourself

❋ There are loads of labyrinths and mazes all over the world, and it's impossible to name them all here.

If you are looking for a labyrinth near where you live or perhaps when on vacation, you can check out the following sites:

**For the USA and Canada:**

www.labyrinthlocator.com/labyrinth-links/categories/1354-usa-canada (there are links here to websites in the USA and Canada, as well as in Europe and throughout the world)

**Interactive labyrinth and maze map for the USA, Canada and Mexico:**

www.wellfedspirit.org/welcome/map-intro/index.html

**For the UK:**

www.labyrinthsinbritain.uk/map-of-uk-labyrinths-mazes

www.westerngeomancy.org/labyrinths-of-the-british-isles

**For Australia:**

www.labyrinths.mountainmakers.com.au

❋ **Summer corn mazes**, planted in cornfields between around July and autumn, are especially popular. Some have even become permanent fixtures. You can find out more about individual corn mazes online.

❋ Some of the most interesting labyrinths and mazes can be found in palace gardens or parks. These are just a few examples:

**The Garden Maze,** Luray Caverns, Luray, Virginia, USA
**Governor's Palace maze,** Williamsburg, Virginia, USA
**Blenheim Palace maze,** Woodstock, England
**The Peace Maze,** Castlewellan, Northern Ireland
(the world's largest perennial hedge maze)
**Longleat Hedge Maze,** Warminster, England
**The Traquair Maze,** Innerleithen, Scotland
**Ashcombe Maze & Lavender Gardens,** Victoria, Australia

# Glossary

**Marine fossils (ammonites)**

P. **26**–28

are sea creatures from prehistoric times. They are mostly petrified and their shells are shaped like a spiral.

**Coriolis force**

P. 27

is named after the French physicist, Gaspard Gustave de Coriolis (1792-1843). This force takes place due to the rotation of the Earth around its axis, which creates huge currents that deflect the winds. The winds then spiral in one direction in the Northern Hemisphere and the opposite direction in the Southern Hemisphere.

**Tarry method**

P. 83

is a system to safely find your way out of a maze. It was named after its discoverer, a Frenchman called Gaston Tarry (1843–1913). He was a financial inspector and was interested in numbers and math.

Library of Congress Control Number: 2021938607
A CIP catalogue record for this book is available from the British Library.

Translated from the German by Paul Kelly

Editorial direction: Doris Kutschbach
Copyediting: Brad Finger
Design, layout, production management: Susanne Hermann
Separations: Reproline Mediateam
Printing and binding: DZS Grafik, d.o.o., Ljubljana, Slovenia
Paper: Amber Graphic

Prestel Publishing compensates the $CO_2$ emissions produced from the making of this book by supporting a reforestation project in Brazil. Find further information on the project here:
www.ClimatePartner.com/14044-1912-1001

Penguin Random House Verlagsgruppe FSC® N001967
ISBN 978-3-7913-7474-1
www.prestel.com